Making a Difference

HARCOURT BRACE SOCIAL STUDIES

ACTIVITY BOOK

HARCOURT BRACE & COMPANY

Orlando Atlanta Austin Boston San Francisco Chicago Dallas

New York Toronto London

Visit The Learning Site at http://www.hbschool.com

The activities in this book reinforce or extend social studies concepts and skills in **MAKING A DIFFERENCE.** There is one activity for each content, skill, or Write-On Chart lesson presented in the Teacher's Edition. Directions for use and reproductions of completed pages appear in the Teacher's Edition within the Close of each lesson.

CONTENTS

WRITE-ON CHARTS

Name _____ Date _____

Class Jobs

Read the story. Draw a line under the main idea.
Circle one detail of the story. Answer the questions.

> Each child in Mrs. Gray's class has
> a job to do. Mary waters the plants.
> John empties the trash. Alice cleans
> the erasers. Bob and Mike keep the
> room neat. When we all do our jobs,
> our classroom is a better place.

1. Who waters the plants? _____

2. What makes the classroom a better place? _____

_____

Name _____ Date _____

Helping Hands

In the first box, draw a picture of you helping your family at home. In the second box, draw a picture of someone in your community helping you.

I help at home.

Others help me.

Make a Map

This picture shows how a classroom looks from above.

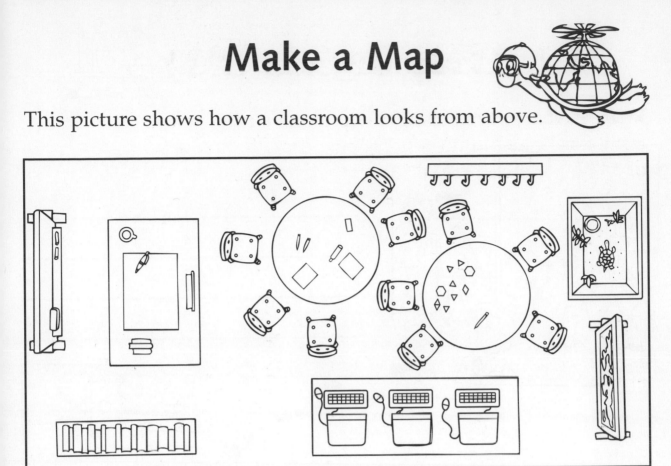

Draw a map of the classroom using shapes and colors.

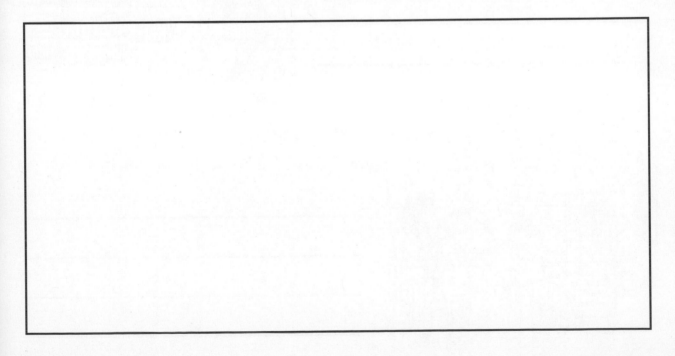

My Trip to the City

Write in this journal about a trip to the city.

_____

_____

_____

_____

_____

_____

_____

_____

_____

_____

_____

Finish the Map

Draw symbols in the map key. Use your symbols to make the map. Write a title. Use the compass rose to write two questions about your map.

_____

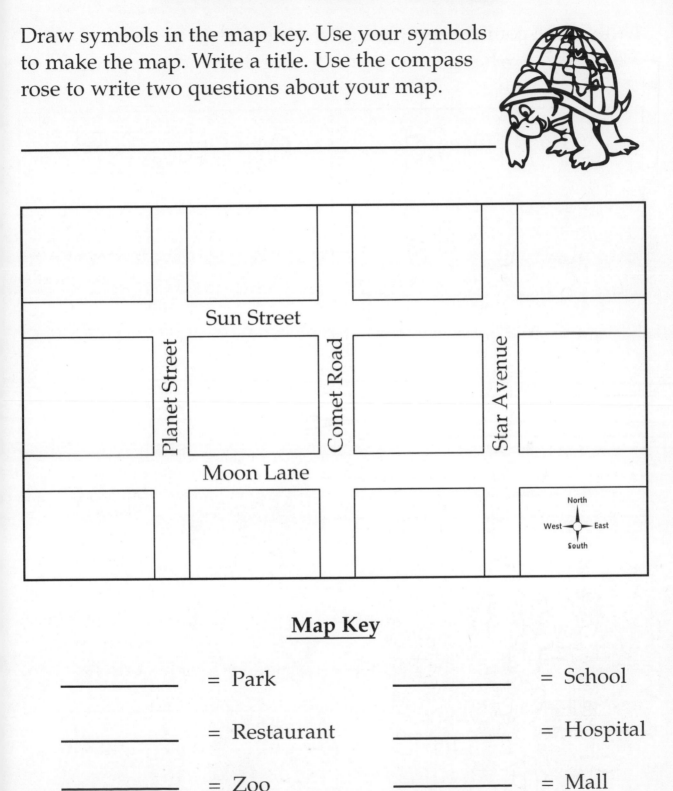

Map Key

_____ = Park   _____ = School

_____ = Restaurant   _____ = Hospital

_____ = Zoo   _____ = Mall

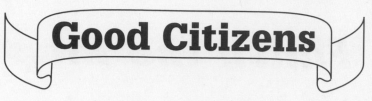

Good Citizens

Look at the pictures and clues at the bottom of the page.
Make lists of what good citizens <u>do</u> and <u>do not</u> do.

Good Citizens Do	Good Citizens Do Not

respect
others'
property.

respect
their
country.

care for
the Earth.

care about
others.

litter.

fight.

Name _____   Date _____

Pop-Up Scenes

Color and cut out one of the scenes. Fold to display it. Make rocks, trees, or plants to place in front of the scene.

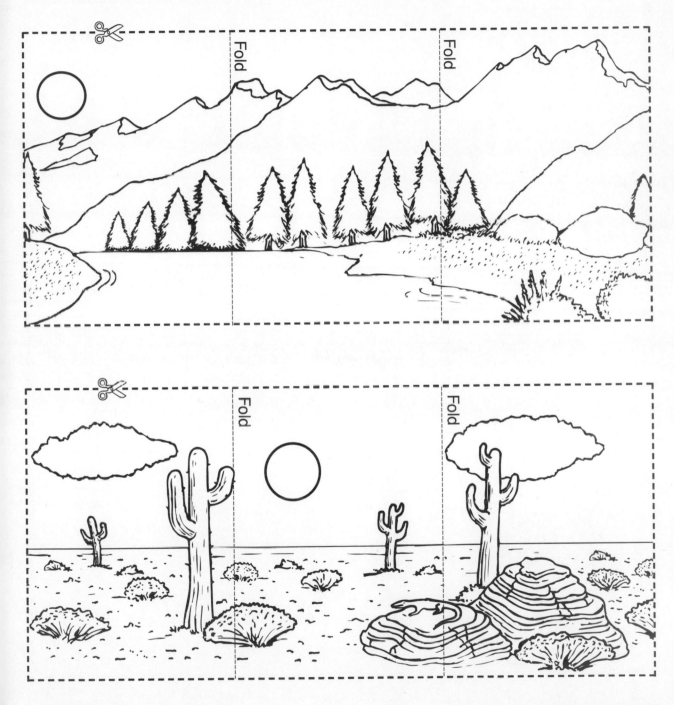

Use with Unit 2, Lesson 1.

Find Land and Water

Use crayons to color the symbols in the map key.
Then follow the map key to color the land and
water on the map.

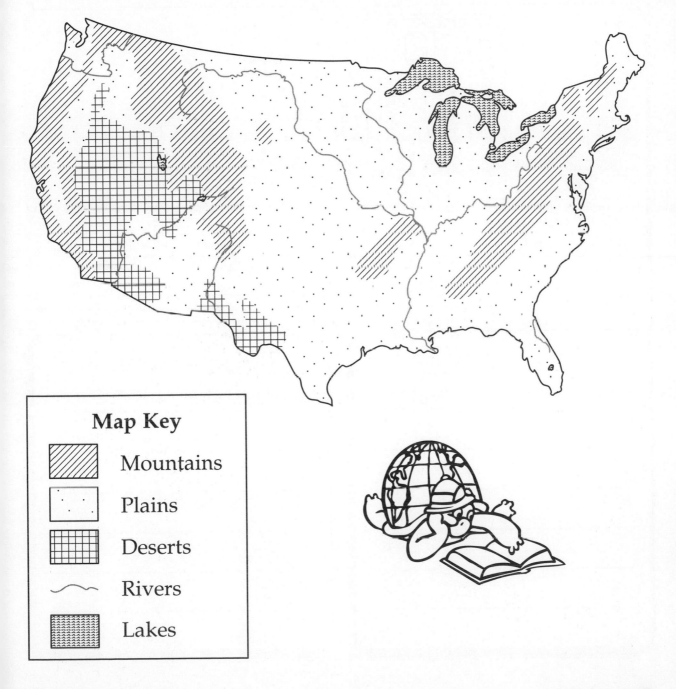

Map Key

▨	Mountains
▫	Plains
▦	Deserts
∿	Rivers
▦	Lakes

What Should I Pack?

What would you pack if you were going to Florida in the summer? What would you pack if you were going to Colorado in the winter? Make two lists.

Things for Florida	Things for Colorado
_____	_____
_____	_____
_____	_____
_____	_____
_____	_____
_____	_____

Where in the World Is It?

Write the letter of each place in the small circle nearest the place on the map.

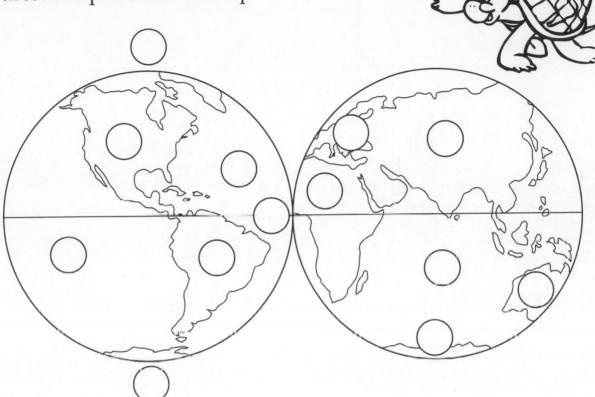

A. Africa

B. Antarctica

C. Asia

D. Atlantic Ocean

E. Australia

F. equator

G. Europe

H. Indian Ocean

I. North America

J. North Pole

K. Pacific Ocean

L. South America

M. South Pole

Name _____   Date _____

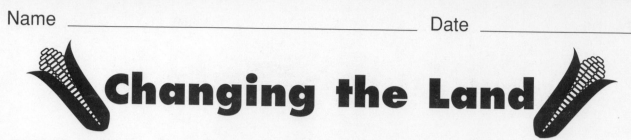

Changing the Land

Color each picture. Write the numbers 1 to 6 to put
the pictures in the correct order. Write a caption for
each picture.

_____   _____   _____

_____   _____   _____

Oranges to Orange Juice

Complete the flow chart. Draw pictures or write sentences. Draw arrows to finish your chart.

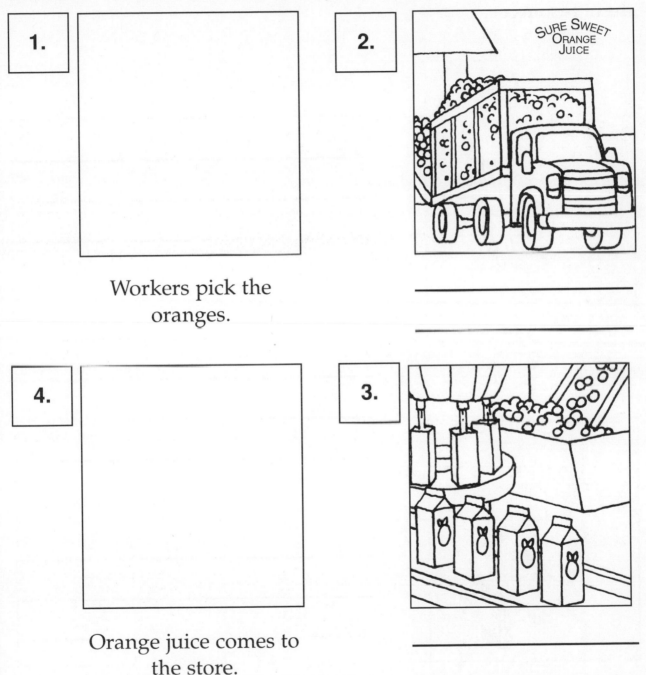

1.

Workers pick the oranges.

2. SURE SWEET ORANGE JUICE

_____

4.

Orange juice comes to the store.

3.

_____

Using Resources

Look at the resources on the left. Write about
things at your home that are made from
these resources.

1.

_____

_____

_____

_____

2.

_____

_____

_____

_____

3.

_____

_____

_____

_____

Resource Table

1. Underline the title of this table.
2. Circle the resources used in making soap.
3. Make an **X** next to each good made from apples.
4. Add one of these resources to the table. Draw and label it.
   tomatoes   chickens   grapes   cows
5. On the table, draw and label at least two goods that come from the resource.

From Resources to Goods

Resource	Goods		
corn	cereal	soap	margarine
apples	juice	sauce	pie
sheep	leather	wool	soap
peanuts	peanut butter	soap	animal food

Rules of the Forest

Circle people who are not using the forest wisely.
Then write rules for keeping the forest clean and safe.

**Please Obey
the Rules**

_____
_____
_____
_____
_____
_____

Name _____ Date _____

People Give Services

In each box, draw a picture of someone
doing a community service.

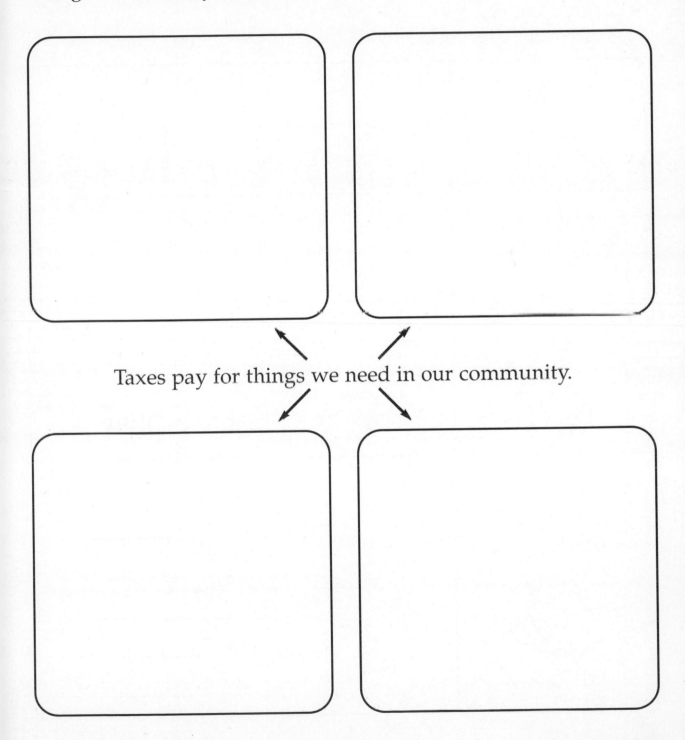

Taxes pay for things we need in our community.

Desk Pictograph

How many of these things are in your desk? Use tally marks or other symbols to show how many of each you have.

Name _____   Date _____

Making a Shirt

Complete the chart by adding words or pictures
to show how a shirt is made.

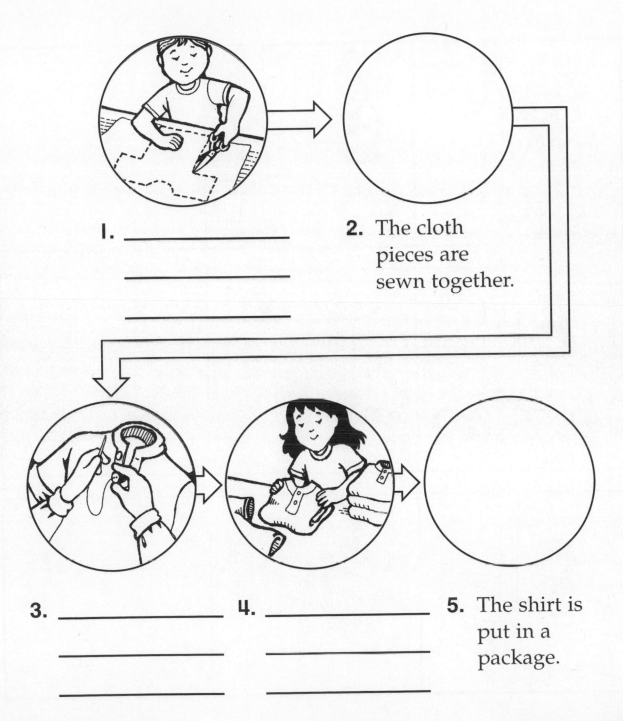

1. _____
_____
_____

2. The cloth pieces are sewn together.

3. _____
_____
_____

4. _____
_____
_____

5. The shirt is put in a package.

Predict What Will Happen

Draw or write an ending for each story. Show what
you predict will happen next.

A Good Trade

Help Su Li and Mary trade something they have a lot of for something they need. Cut out and paste one good from each person to make a fair trade. Write why each was a fair trade.

pencils   erasers   crayons

erasers   pencils   crayons

What's in the Box?

You have just been shopping. Draw a picture to show what you bought. Then write a paragraph to tell where you bought it, who produced or made it, and how you paid for it.

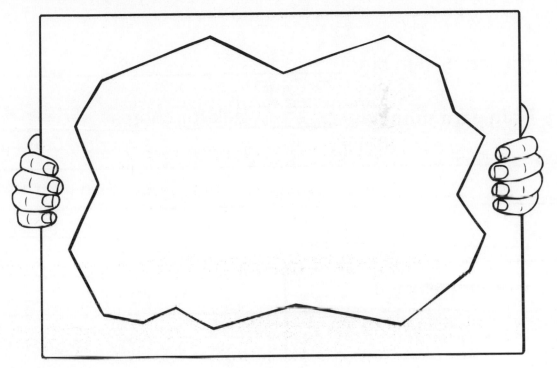

_____

_____

_____

_____

_____

_____

_____

Saving Money

Think of something you would like to buy that costs $20.
Imagine that you get $5 a week for doing chores. Think of
other ways to earn money. Use the table to make a plan.
Write how long it will take you to save the money you need.

Goal   To earn $20 to buy _____

Ways I can earn money _____ $5 a week for chores _____

_____

_____

Money earned	Money spent

It will take me _____ to save the money.

Name _____ Date _____

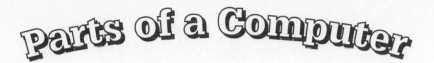

Parts of a Computer

Answer the questions about the computer
by looking at the diagram.

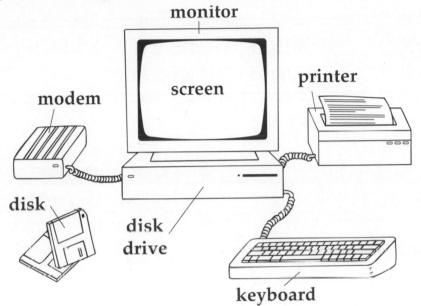

1. What part do you use to type in words?

_____

2. What part do you use to see your work on paper?

_____

3. What are two parts that are connected to the disk drive?

_____

4. In what part do you find the screen?

_____

Puzzling Words

Choose a word from the box that fits each clue. Write the letters on the lines.

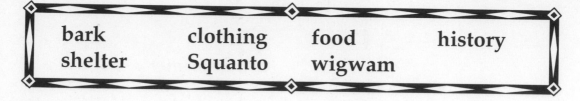

bark   clothing   food   history
shelter   Squanto   wigwam

1. Stories that people tell about the past
2. An Indian who helped the Pilgrims
3. The things people eat

4. One kind of Indian shelter
5. What wigwams are made of
6. The things people wear
7. The homes people live in

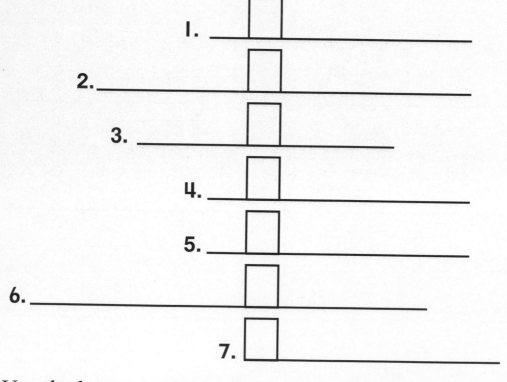

Use the letters in the boxes to fill in the sentence.

The _____ were the first Americans.

Use with Unit 4, Lesson 1.

Name _____ Date _____

Use a Time Line to Tell a Story

Mike's time line shows what happens over
four months. Write a story about the things
that happen.

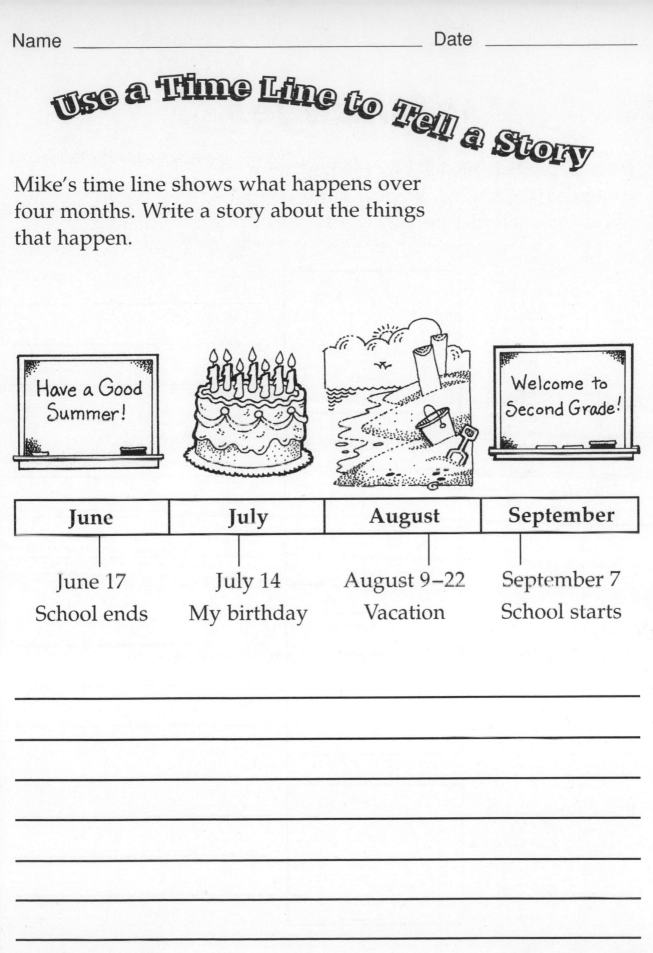

June	July	August	September
June 17	July 14	August 9–22	September 7
School ends	My birthday	Vacation	School starts

_____

_____

_____

_____

_____

_____

Changes

Draw a picture in each box to show how
things have changed. Write a sentence to
tell about each picture.

Old Town/New Town

Cut out the pictures and paste them on the map to
show how Old Town has changed.

Old Town, 1773

New Town, Today

Name _____ Date _____

All About Our Community

Make a cover for a book about your community. Finish the title. Draw a picture of a landmark, a special feature, or an important person to show what is special about your community.

All About

_____

Cause and Effect

Look at each cause. Draw its effect.

Write a Picture Story

Washington, D.C., has many famous landmarks. Cut out the pictures and paste them on drawing paper. Write a story about a trip to our nation's capital.

Make a Grid Picture

Complete the grid by filling in letters and numbers.
Color the listed squares to make a picture.

Yellow: A-6, A-7
Black: B-4, C-2, C-3, C-4, C-5, C-6, D-1, D-2,
D-3, D-4, D-5, D-6, D-7
Red: E-2, E-6, F-2, F-6, G-2, G-3, G-4, G-5, G-6

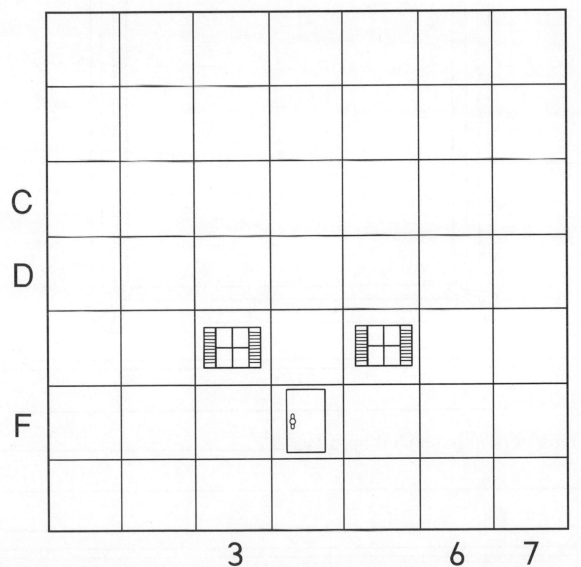

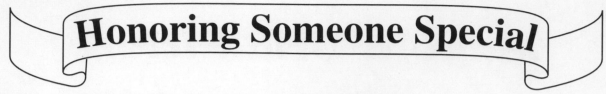

Honoring Someone Special

Draw a picture of someone who is making history today. Write who the person is and why he or she is special.

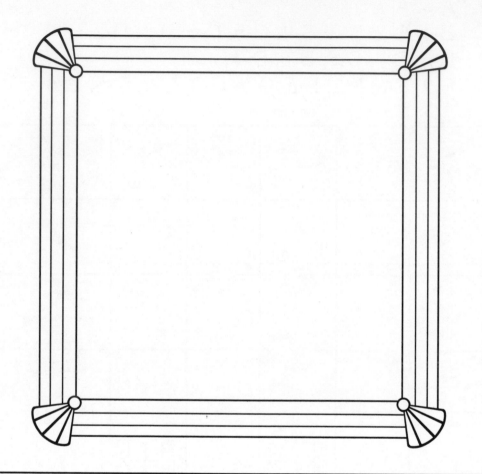

This is _____.

This person is special because _____

_____

_____.

I Am an American

Complete each sentence.

The name of my country is _____

_____ .

A symbol of my country is _____ .

A famous person in my country's history is _____

_____ .

This person is famous because _____

_____ .

Something I do to honor my country is _____

_____

_____ .

Vote for a Class Trip

The children in Class 2A are planning a trip.

Should they go to the zoo?

Should they go to a museum?

The children vote to decide.

Count the ballots.

Ballot	**Ballot**	**Ballot**	**Ballot**	**Ballot**
zoo ☑ museum ☐	zoo ☑ museum ☐	zoo ☑ museum ☐	zoo ☐ museum ☑	zoo ☐ museum ☑

Ballot	**Ballot**	**Ballot**	**Ballot**	**Ballot**
zoo ☐ museum ☑	zoo ☑ museum ☐	zoo ☐ museum ☑	zoo ☑ museum ☐	zoo ☐ museum ☑

Ballot	**Ballot**	**Ballot**	**Ballot**	**Ballot**
zoo ☑ museum ☐	zoo ☑ museum ☐	zoo ☑ museum ☐	zoo ☐ museum ☑	zoo ☑ museum ☐

_____ children vote for the zoo.

_____ children vote for the museum.

Where will the class go? _____

Name _____   Date _____

Government Crossword

Read the clues down and across. Write words from the box to solve the puzzle.

President	three
Supreme Court	Congress
Constitution	nine

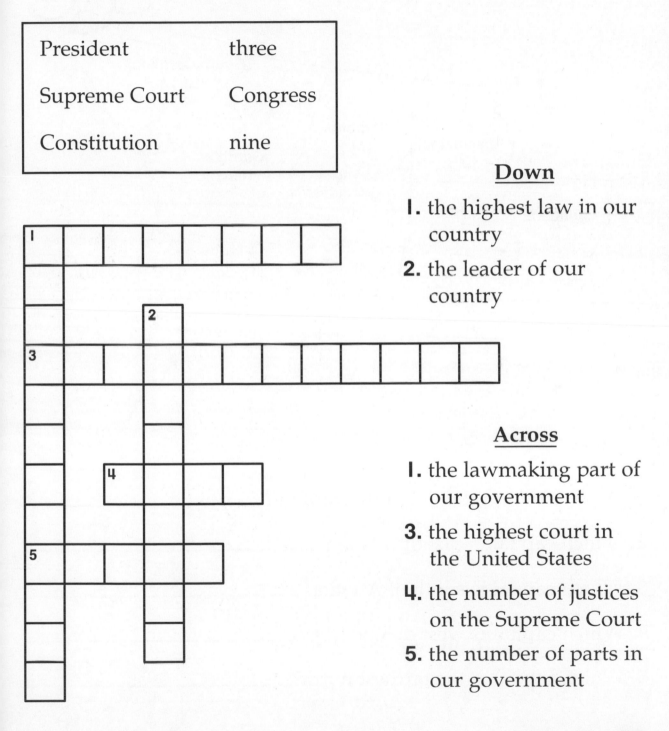

Down

1. the highest law in our country

2. the leader of our country

Across

1. the lawmaking part of our government

3. the highest court in the United States

4. the number of justices on the Supreme Court

5. the number of parts in our government

Name _____   Date _____

Using Directions

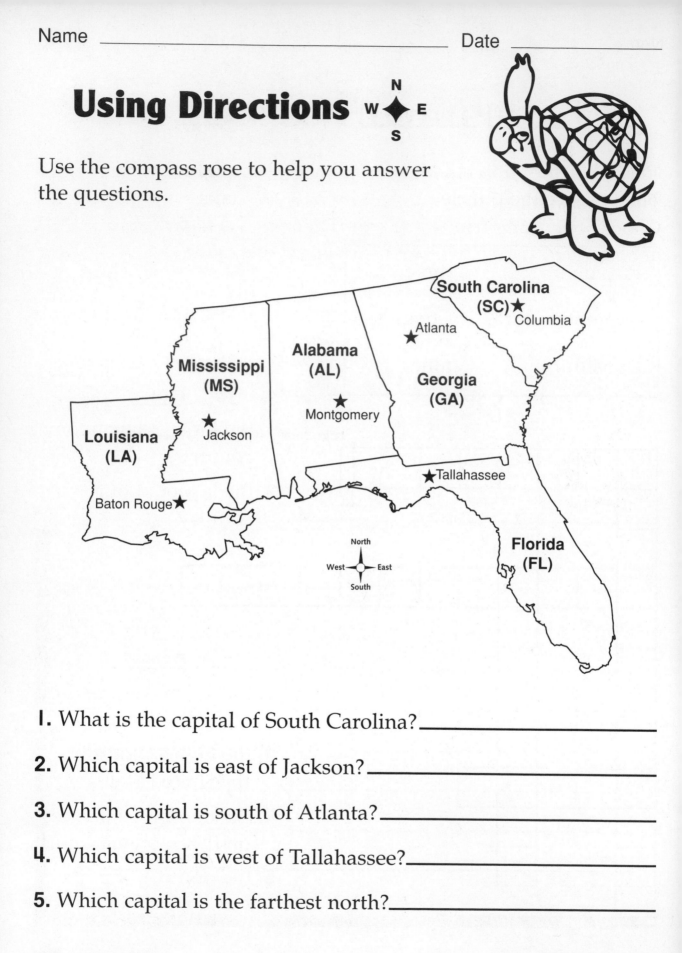

Use the compass rose to help you answer
the questions.

1. What is the capital of South Carolina? _____

2. Which capital is east of Jackson? _____

3. Which capital is south of Atlanta? _____

4. Which capital is west of Tallahassee? _____

5. Which capital is the farthest north? _____

Use with Unit 5, Skill.

Name _____ Date _____

The school board is deciding how to spend money.
These are some of the choices they have to make.
Choose one thing from each pair. Then write a letter
about one of these. Tell the school board why you
would like them to make this choice.

Librarian or Art Teacher?
Band Uniforms or Football Uniforms?
Swings or Stoves?

Fact or Opinion

Write **fact** or **opinion** for each sentence.

1. Pennsylvania is one of the 50 states.

   _____

2. Pennsylvania is the best state to visit.

   _____

3. The city of Philadelphia is in Pennsylvania.

   _____

4. You can see the Liberty Bell in Philadelphia.

   _____

5. The capital of Pennsylvania is Harrisburg.

   _____

6. If you visit Pennsylvania, you should go by airplane.

   _____

Write a fact and an opinion about your state or community.

Fact: _____

_____

Opinion: _____

_____

Freedom Facts

Fill in the blanks. Use words from the box.

1. _____ said, "Give me liberty or give me death."

2. The _____ gives us our freedoms.

3. The _____ is a plan of government for the United States.

4. _____ worked for the rights of African Americans by not giving up her seat on a bus.

5. _____ are the rights people have to make their own choices.

Freedoms

Bill of Rights

Rosa Parks

Patrick Henry

Constitution

On the Move

Pretend you are a pioneer. Fill in the ticket to show where you want to go. Draw a picture of yourself with the way you would use to travel.

Winter Food

Choose a vegetable from the story. Draw a
picture for each step. Then number the boxes
to show the correct order of the steps.

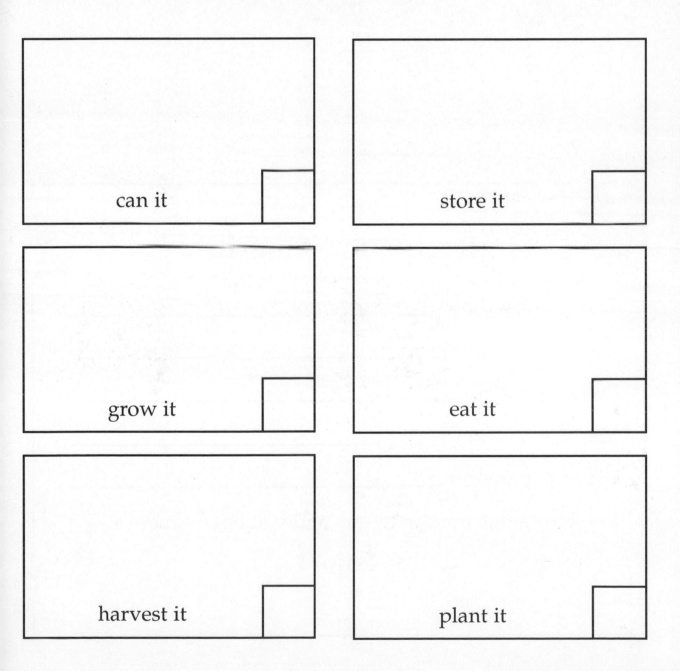

can it	store it
grow it	eat it
harvest it	plant it

Recipe for America

Find names of countries on a globe.
Use them to complete the recipe.

Recipe for America

Take stories from _____.

Add music from _____.

Put in art from _____.

Mix in food from _____.

Stir in games from _____.

Cook for a few hundred years and you have America.

Enjoy!

Name _____ Date _____

How did these children's ancestors come to America? Color in a bar next to each form of transportation for every time it was used.

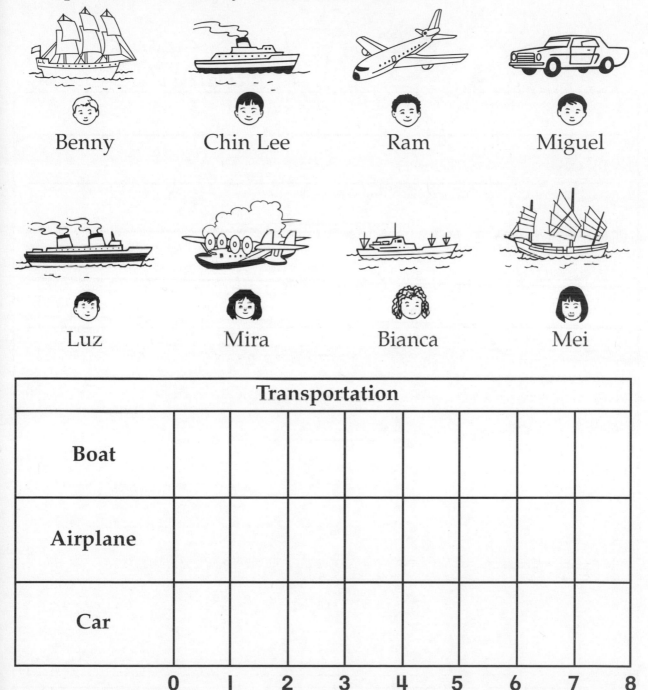

Transportation								
Boat								
Airplane								
Car								

0   1   2   3   4   5   6   7   8

Family Pride

Think of things that older members of your family
have taught you how to do or say. Write them on the
lines below. Then draw a picture of your family.

_____

_____

_____

_____

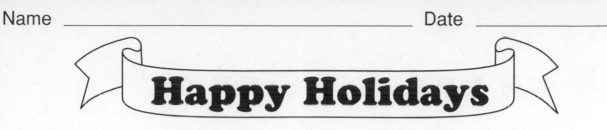

Happy Holidays

Write the name of the holiday below its symbols. In the last box, draw symbols of a celebration in your community. Write the name of the celebration.

1

2

_____

_____

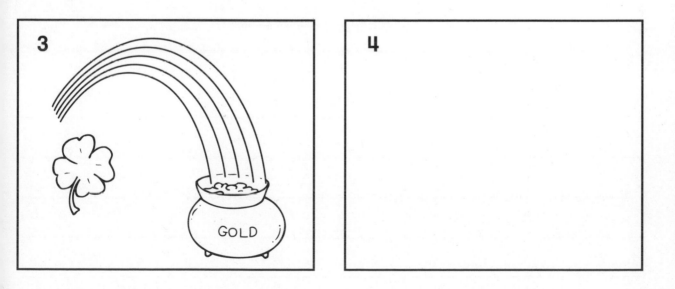

3

GOLD

4

_____

_____

Artifact Clues

What do the artifacts tell you about the people who made and used them? Write about them on the lines.

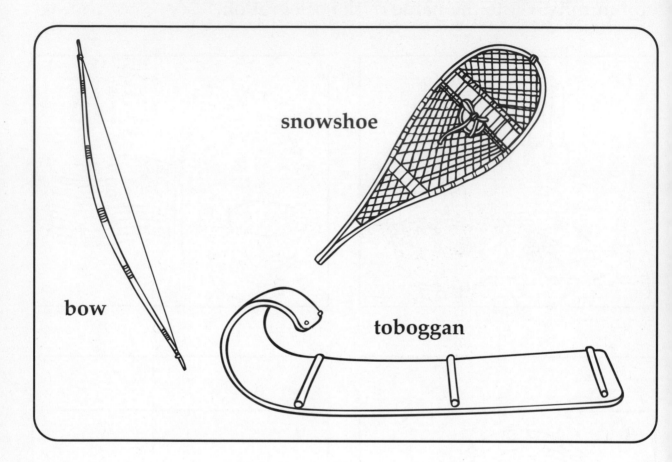

_____

_____

_____

_____

_____

Use with Unit 6, Skill.

Poster Talk

What message do you think the person
who made this poster had in mind?
Write it on the lines.

_____

_____

_____

_____

_____

Name _____ Date _____

Solve the Problem

Find the problem in the picture. Then use
the steps to tell how you would solve it.

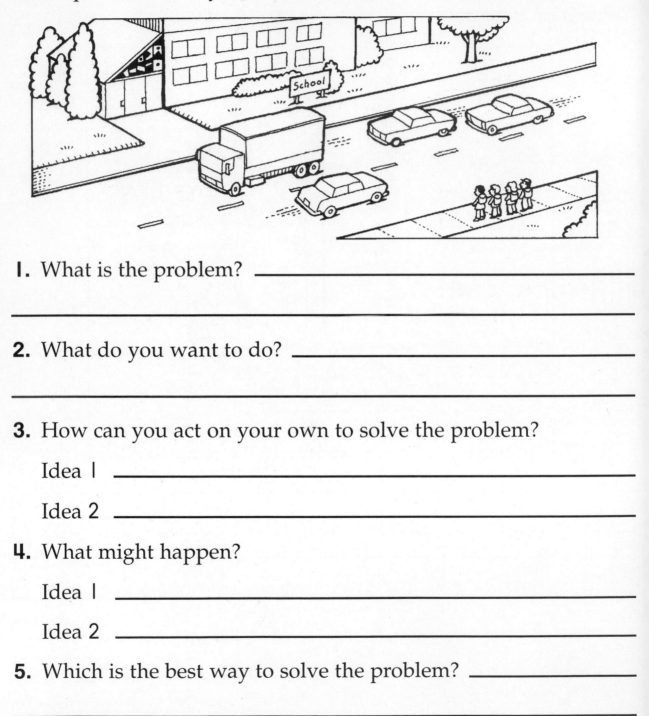

1. What is the problem? _____

_____

2. What do you want to do? _____

_____

3. How can you act on your own to solve the problem?

   Idea 1 _____

   Idea 2 _____

4. What might happen?

   Idea 1 _____

   Idea 2 _____

5. Which is the best way to solve the problem? _____

_____

Use with Unit 6, Skill.

Name _____ Date _____

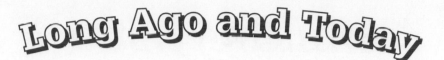
Long Ago and Today

Write a story below the pictures to tell how things
have changed.

Long ago. . .

_____

_____

_____

_____

But today. . .

_____

_____

_____

_____

Use with Write-On Chart 1.   Activity Book **53**

☆ *Making Laws* ☆

Circle each person who is following a safety law.
Write laws to match the pictures you circled.

Laws

_____

_____

_____

_____

Use with Write-On Chart 2.

Name _____ Date _____

Symbols All Around Us

Write **S** on the line if the symbol is for a safety law.
Write **I** if it is for information.

1.

2.

HOSPITAL

3.

R R

4.

5.

STOP

6.

BIKE PATH

7.

BUS
STOP

8.

GAS

9.

Write a Picture Story

Nu Dang lives in Bangkok, Thailand. On another sheet of paper, write a story to go along with the pictures.

Transportation

Home

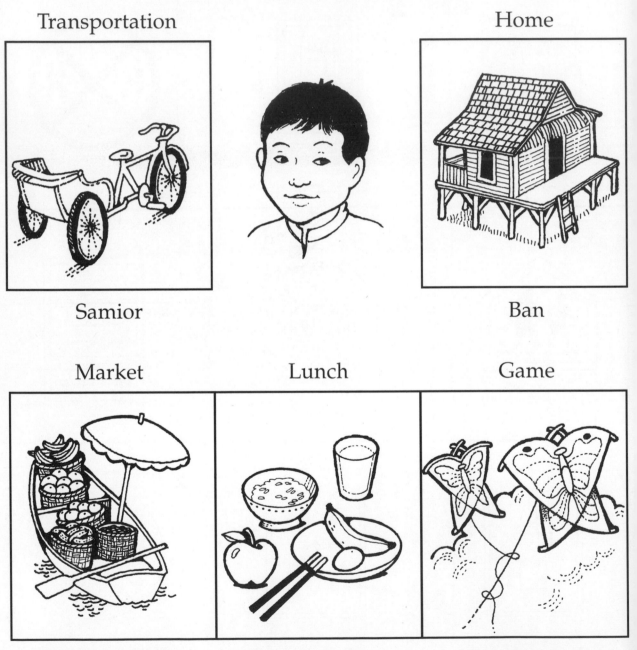

Samior

Ban

Market

Lunch

Game

Floating Market

Rice, Fish, Fruit

Kite Fighting

Name _____ Date _____

What Belongs Where?

Draw a line from each home to where it belongs.

Name ______________________________ Date ______________

Using Water

Draw pictures or write about how you use water at home, at school, and at play.

Home

School

Play

Use with Write-On Chart 6.

Name _____ Date _____

Goods and Resources

Which are goods and which are resources?
List the words below in the correct boxes. Then
draw lines from the resources to the goods made

Resources	Goods

cotton   cows   hamburger   bread

peanut butter   jeans   wheat   shirts

trees   pencils   tomatoes   raisins

tomato soup   milk   peanuts   grapes

Use with Write-On Chart 7.   Activity Book **59**

Reduce, Reuse, Recycle!

Write sentences to tell how to reduce, reuse, or recycle each thing.

Mailing a Letter

Fill in the envelope with your name and address and the name and address of a friend. Then number the pictures from I to 6 to show how a letter gets from you to a friend.

From

_____

_____

_____

To

_____

_____

_____

Plan a Business

You are planning to open a restaurant. Give it a name, and fill in the business plan. List the costs. Tell where your restaurant will be and who will come to eat there.

My Business Plan

Costs _____

_____

Location _____

_____

Customers _____

_____

Use with Write-On Chart 10.

Name _____ Date _____

Go Shopping

Welcome to the Kids' Flea Market. What goods
and services will you buy? Tell why.

_____

_____

_____

_____

_____

_____

Name _____   Date _____

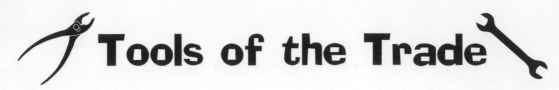

Tools of the Trade

Look at the tools. List two workers who would use each tool in their jobs.

Use with Write-On Chart 12.

Then and Now

Draw a picture of yourself in the space to the right.
List ways you are like the early Americans.
List ways you are different from them.

Different

Alike

Different

Old and New

Choose and circle one picture that shows an old way to do a job. Then draw a picture that shows how this job is done today.

Use with Write-On Chart 14.

Adding Something New

Draw a picture of something you would add
to each museum.

Museum of Natural History

National Museum of
American History

Air and Space Museum

My Dream

Make the outline into a picture of yourself.
Write what your dream for the world is.

Good Citizens Scramble

Unscramble the letters and write the things good citizens do. Then write a letter to match a picture to each word.

1. ☐

e t o v

_ _ _ _

2. ☐

h o n o r   t h e   g f a l

_ _ _ _

3. ☐

p e l h   o t h e r s

_ _ _ _

4. ☐

h e l p   t h e   a e h r t

_ _ _ _ _

A

B Ballots

C Recycle

D STOP

Make a Diagram

Write the words in the school where they belong on the diagram. Their order from top to bottom should show the order of authority.

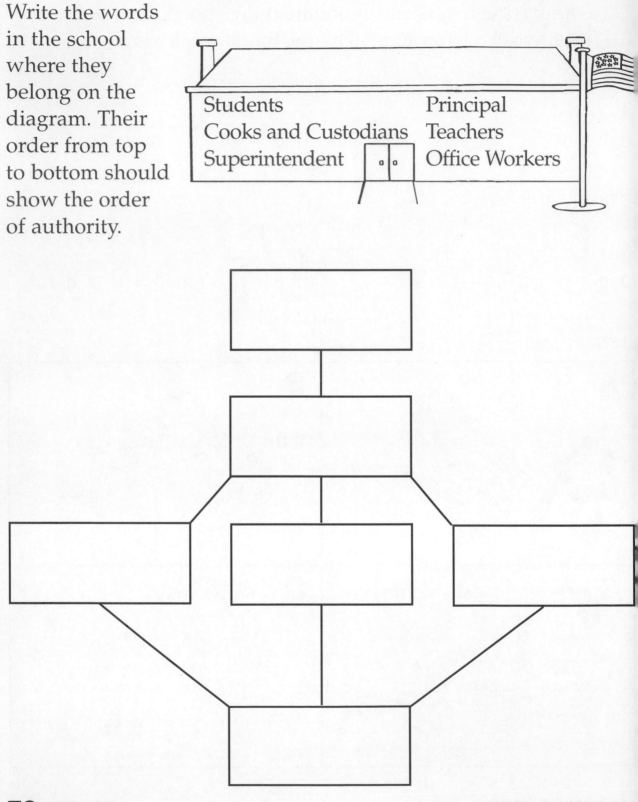

Students
Cooks and Custodians
Superintendent

Principal
Teachers
Office Workers

Name _____ Date _____

State Flag Facts

Here are some facts about four state flags. Read the
facts. Then use the code to write the name of each state.

A	B	C	D	E	F	G	H	I	J	K	L	M
1	2	3	4	5	6	7	8	9	10	11	12	13

N	O	P	Q	R	S	T	U	V	W	X	Y	Z
14	15	16	17	18	19	20	21	22	23	24	25	26

1. This state's flag shows eight gold stars. Seven stars are in the
shape of the Big Dipper. The eighth is the North Star—a
symbol that this state is located farthest north.
1   12   1   19   11   1

___ ___ ___ ___ ___ ___ ___

2. A shield on this state's flag shows symbols of farming—wheat,
an ear of corn, and an ox. Under the shield is the date this
state became the first state.
4   5   12   1   23   1   18   5

___ ___ ___ ___ ___ ___ ___ ___

3. A lot of diamonds come from this state. That's what the
diamond-shaped design on this flag tells people.
1   18   11   1   14   19   1   19

___ ___ ___ ___ ___ ___ ___ ___

4. Red and yellow rays on this flag stand for the setting sun.
1   18   9   26   15   14   1

___ ___ ___ ___ ___ ___ ___

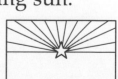

Freedom Match

Draw a line to match each picture with a freedom or right.

1. freedom of speech

2. freedom to report the news

3. freedom of religion

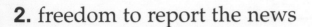

4. freedom of groups to meet

5. right to a fair trial

A Letter from the West

Write to a friend or family member back home.
Tell about your wagon journey west.

_____ , 1841

Dear _____ ,

_____

_____

_____

_____

_____

_____

_____

_____

_____

_____ ,

_____

Country Quiz

Look at the map to find each country below. Write your answer on the line.

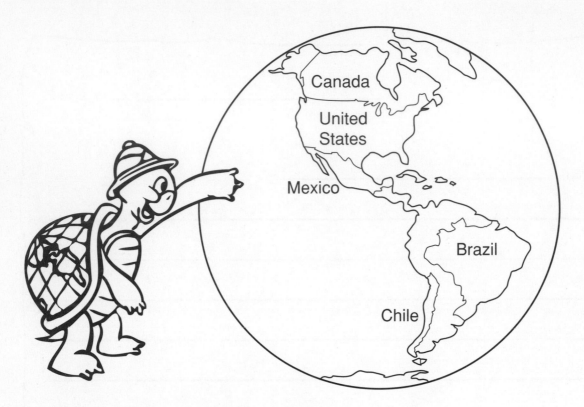

1. The highest mountains in South America are in a very long, narrow country. _____

2. The largest country in South America has the world's largest river, the Amazon. _____

3. Our largest neighbor is the country to the north of us. _____

4. Corn is an important crop for our nearest neighbor to the south. _____

Celebration Invitation

Think of a celebration you would like to have.
Draw a picture and fill out the invitation for
your celebration. Cut out the invitation and
give it to a friend.

You Are Invited!

Come to our _____
celebration.

Given by _____

Date _____

Time _____

Place _____

Stitching a Story

Mandy stitched a picture to tell about herself and her family. Write a paragraph to tell about Mandy and her family.

_____

_____

_____

_____

_____